Breaking A

GW00374687

How can you build a location independent lifestyle in 2023?

Season One: Spring 2023

S. Calvin Jones

Wild Writer Publishing, June 2023

Contents

Preface

Before I introduce this book, I should stress one point. I am a single, nearly-middle-aged man. I don't have a family. I don't have a mortgage. This means I'm in a relatively fortuitous position, without some of the ties that bind people to a job and a place.

The approach I'm going to take to attempt to *Break Free in 2023* will not be viable for everyone. But it will be viable for some. And I hope the general approach I report within this book series, and my successes and failures, have broader appeal. If you're looking into ways to earn multiple streams of income and to become location independent, experiences and lessons reported in this book series will, I'm sure, be of some use.

This is the first volume of a three-volume series I'm writing in 2023. It covers the winter-into-spring season, January-April 2023. The summer volume (May-August 2023) will appear in early September and the autumn-into-winter volume will take us to the finishing line, covering September-December.

1 Introduction

It's early January 2023. I'm sitting in a cafe in Falmouth, a town in Cornwall in the far south west of England. It's mild but ceaselessly wet and drizzly.

Typical English winter weather.

I'm pondering life. What's next?

We've all been through the trauma of a global pandemic. It's taken many lives. Our collective reaction to it has *changed* many lives, too. Enforced home-working cut out the commute for many and created new habits and new expectations.

Some have asked: *is the traditional office commute strictly necessary?*

Home working has achieved prominence as a response to lockdowns and a much contested means to slow the spread of the virus.

Many people emerged from the trauma of lockdowns with a fresh outlook. Some people, and the companies they work for, discovered the feasibility of remote working. Some tested the practicalities of remote working from anywhere, not just home.

Many people just wanted to get back to the office. To the social life. To the lunchtime stroll to the local cafe and the after-work drink with colleagues. To *contact* with other people.

Others faced a more fundamental question, literally: *is the juice* (a house with a mortgage, loads of stuff accumulated in that house, a sedentary lifestyle) really *worth the squeeze* (of the London Underground or daily car commute, the confines of office cell, and the minimal freedom)?

Many on furlow took to YouTube, discovering new ways to make a living online. Many self-published novels are the children of lockdowns.

Things changed after 2019.

And so I found myself pondering these sorts of questions. By the start of 2023 an idea began to form. Cornwall is beautiful, sure. But it can be bleak in winter.

I couldn't dislodge a question on my mind: *do I really need to endure another temperate zone winter*?

As a nature lover, I'm acutely aware that the closer one gets to the equator, the tropics, the richer, more exuberant, the plant and animal life gets. If you're a naturalist, you're fuelled by the richness of nature. You need to spend as much time as possible close to and within the tropics, or you wilt.

I needed to be in nature. That demanded location independence. Could I find a new lifestyle that made location independence possible? Earning an income via online ventures? Maybe small amounts of income from multiple avenues that added up to a full-time income?

A few years before the pandemic I discovered the world of book writing and independent book publishing. Writing fitted well with my favoured lifestyle. I like to sit on the veranda of a rainforest lodge, with my computer, drinking coffee, thinking, looking, writing short pieces for my blog about the nature that lifts my spirits.

Maybe I could write books, too?

The next question was, thus: *could book sales yield an income to help make that sort of lifestyle viable?*

Vanlife was and remains all the rage. *The* trendy lifestyle.

Back in February 2018, around the time I discovered book self-publishing, I purchased, and moved into, an old Citroen Berlingo van.

Hardcore! Berlingos are *tiny*. Even by European standards that's a pretty small van. To many of my friends, I'd lost the plot. To me, I'd found my plot: a mobile beach-side tiny home.

Used at the time to the more conventional house-life, I still wonder what possessed me to move into that van. I was in Cornwall. Many surfers live in vans in Cornwall. Maybe that was it?

Well, not really. At the time, I was crashing in a backpackers hostel. I quite liked 'roughing it' and meeting new people as they passed through on their travels. I'd embraced that dirtbag lifestyle a few years earlier during a four-month stay in Cambodia. Hammock-life was even more hardcore than Berlingo vanlife!

And I was studying ecology at the nearby Exeter University, Penryn Campus. So I was running out of money.

By that time, I was what might best be described as a 'nearing-middle-aged professional' with over two decades of employment to my name. I'd done some relatively useful stuff in my chosen field, nature conservation. I held some promise for promotion within organisations I loved, pursuing a mission I was totally dedicated to.

I seemed relatively well cut out for a career as a cog in the great beastly machine that is the nature conservation sector.

But this move of mine, into a van, was perhaps the first hint that my lifestyle would take a rather odd and unconventional turn.

After a few years in my van, noting my dramatic reduction in costs, I began to wonder if I might have found a key part of my niche.

Dramatically reduced day-to-day living costs yielded a dramatically increased amount of free time. Might this thereby provide the 'head space' I needed to write books and independently publish them? Could they actually sell? Would they generate just enough income to buy one of my daily coffees? Or could independently published book sales provide a more appreciable income?

And were there additional ways of earning money online to supplement that income? Could all this enable me to escape the stultifying, constraining indignity of conventional employment in drizzly England?

Could I really become a 'digital nomad'?

Digital nomads often work punishingly hard on a variety of side hustles. They seek to build up multiple streams of income.

'Passive' income frequently demands an awful lot of unpaid work upfront before one has a product that might go on to sell without much additional effort (i.e. 'passively'). One usually needs a conventional job on the side to fund oneself as they buildup their side business.

Independently publishing books is far from passive: it does, after all, require one to first write those books!

If it's possible to first dramatically reduce one's lifestyle costs, at least initially, a relatively modest side income or two may well constitute all that's needed to get a digital nomad lifestyle off the ground. One can then slowly ramp-up the income.

This relaxing form of location independent digital nomadism, or digital minimalism, has a more succinct name: Flowmadism.

This is a term I first picked up from a YouTube video by a chap called Tom Torero. Tom sadly passed away recently and had a slightly controversial history as a dating coach.

In that video Tom set out how one might combine minimalism, side incomes and nomadism to create a relatively relaxed, location independent lifestyle.

That's Flowmadism. It's the art of viably living foot-loose and fancy-free if you like.

Back to early January 2023.

I decided that 2023 will be the year I attempt to make low-cost digital nomadism - flowmadism - my way of life.

I decided I'd write a diary of my endeavours. This short 'Breaking Free in 2023: Season One' book represents Volume One of my journey.

It provides a real-world, near-real-time account of my quest during 2023 to break free from the shackles of humdrum UK life and launch my future as a relaxed flowmad.

This volume covers the start of 2023 leading into Spring. That's January, February, March, and April. I'll write the volumes during 2023, representing winter-spring, summer, autumn-winter.

I want to live in the tropics, Asia or Latin America, during the drab English winters, and in the UK or elsewhere in Europe during the European spring, summer and autumn. I want to set up a small wildlife conservation charity supporting nature reserve creation by communities in the tropics.

How do I get myself into a position whereby I have sufficient income, generated from anywhere in the world, to keep myself going during these endeavours? What tools and new skills will I need to ensure it works?

In this first season I'm naive. I've earned all my income to date via fixed-location employment. A cog in someone else's wheel. So I currently know little about running a business, generating a liveable income, and setting up a non-profit charity, least of all while surviving on a location independent or a 'passive' income. The thought of establishing multiple streams of income is somewhat daunting.

The following is my account of that first season, as it unfolded.

Read on to see how Season One has gone!

2 Embracing minimalism

People often ask 'How much do you need to earn?'

I prefer a prior question: 'How little can I live on?'

If I can keep my overall living costs down to a reasonable minimum, I don't need to earn as much. That buys me free time.

Getting myself into a position where I can live on a lot less cash than has hitherto been the case will presumably greatly increase the probability that I can break free of the need for formal employment.

I've already gone a long way to minimising my costs. I live in a tiny van, after all!

Even so, I'm very well aware that I still spend more money each day than I really need to.

I enjoy drinking coffee, for example. And I buy these coffees in local cafés. Why? Because I like writing in cafés overlooking the sea. I use their Wi-Fi. I'm always on the internet and I watch a lot of YouTube videos. This is how I'm learning. It's how I do my research. I watch videos on digital nomadism. I watch videos on independent book publishing. Unfortunately I can't just sit in cafés using their Wi-Fi without buying frequent cups of coffee! So, my biggest expenditure each day is on tea and coffee. I need to change that.

My van has very little space. I don't have any storage elsewhere. All of my belongings exist either in the van or in the cloud. Over the decades I'd built up a monumentally huge library of nature books. Then, starting in 2019, I gradually donated the lot to students at Exeter University. All my remaining books, or at least most of them, are now stored in the cloud and read on my Kindle app on my mobile phone.

I cook most of my meals in the van. I have a small propane gas stove. I've become quite industrious with my cooking.

Although I think of myself as a nomadic vandweller, in reality I tend to stay in one place for a long time. This, too, cuts my costs. I live either on the Isle of Wight or down in Cornwall. I don't travel between the two especially frequently. I'm currently spending probably half the year in Cornwall and the other half on the Isle of Wight. This relative immobility reduces costs.

All told, my daily costs in recent years have probably averaged about £30.

That's already substantially less than most peoples' costs. I'm starting with that advantage.

Can I cut my cost further?

3 Financial viability

It's all very well being minimalist, but one can't live entirely cost-free. I will actually need some sort of income. I need some sort of plan for later in life, too, when I start to slow down and get those aches, pains and probably dementia! I'm not getting any younger…

How much do I actually need to live a happy existence?

There's the day-to-day costs. Food, drink, laundry, those sorts of things. There's the gadgets and subscriptions I need to operate, and those that bring me fun, like Prime Movie. There's the Council Tax contribution.

Then there's traveling itself.

I obviously won't take the van when I head for the tropics. So I'll need to pay for accommodation. In Asia, I might try living from a motorbike and hammock. I slept in a hammock most nights during field work in Cambodia. A return to hammock-life is quite an enticing prospect, for now at least.

One early task will be to write down a detailed daily, weekly, monthly, and yearly budget. That should cover my current average expenditure and my anticipated daily spend once I've fully broken free.

4 Setting a Goal and targets

What's my overall 2023 Goal? Basically, I want to get myself in a position by the end of 2023 where I'm earning a reasonable, largely passive, income, and to be able to live where I like anywhere in the world. Ideally I'd be able to head for the tropics in mid November 2023.

Let's express the Goal more precisely, as if it's already true:

GOAL: *I have sufficient income that I'm able to generate from anywhere globally, and I can choose where I live within reason and without unmanageable risks or constraints.*

That's a lofty Goal for a cubicle drone like me, used to the comforts of employment and an office to commute to.

To bring that Goal to fruition, I need to set some precise *targets*, and I need some specific *actions* so I can track my progress with each target.

Let's set some targets for the whole of 2023 first:

Target 1: write and publish at least five books.

Target 2: set up and monetise a YouTube channel.

Target 3: minimise my expenditure, while still living a good life.

Target 4: be in a position to live in the tropics from mid November 2023

Having set out some whole-year targets that should ensure I achieve my overall Goal, I now need to hone down a bit and specify targets and actions for the first season, spring 2023, January-April.

Over the next four months I will…

Spring Target 1.1: Complete one book manuscript

Spring Target 1.2: Achieve 100 subscribers on my writing YouTube channel

Spring Target 1.3: Reduce spending to £10/day

Spring Target 1.4: Write a more detailed delivery plan to demonstrate how it's possible

to be in a position to live in the tropics from mid-November 2023.

I now have a set of four targets to achieve by the end of April 2023. Let's define some specific actions I'll need to undertake to accomplish those targets. I'll define one or more actions for each target.

Target 1.1 Actions: write book manuscript

1.1.a. Master voice-to-text dictation to write the manuscript

1.1.b. Write at least 1000 words per day

1.1.c. Complete 30,000 word manuscript by end of April

Target 1.2 Actions: build the YouTube channel

1.2.a. Produce a banner for my writer YouTube channel

1.2.b. Produce a decent channel avatar image

1.2.c. Work out how to produce decent video thumbnails

1.2.d. Experiment with producing regular short form videos

1.2.e. Upload at least one video per week

Target 1.3 Actions: reduce spending
1.3.a. Reduce purchased drinks from seven per day to 3 per day

1.3.b. Audit all online subscriptions

1.3.c. Cancel unnecessary subscriptions

1.3.d. Cook all my own food in the van

Target 1.4 Actions: write delivery plan
1.4.a. Just write it!

There we have it.

I wrote the above in mid January 2023. I'll return to those targets and actions at the end of the book, writing in late April, to review how things went.

Next, I'll consider the two initial passive income routes I'll be pursuing, and skills and tools I anticipate I'll need to make them real.

5 Building multiple streams of income

Okay, so I have a Goal and some targets and actions set out.

I know roughly what my daily, weekly, monthly and yearly costs might be after I've managed to break free by the end of 2023. I'll need a budget for travelling between locations, then I'll have daily spending.

I'll assume an annual budget of £5,000 to travel between locations. Initially, I need to reduce my daily expenditure to £10. That's £70 per week, £280 per month, £3360 per year to cover day-to-day spending. That's extreme frugality! But, because I'm living in a van in the UK, I think it's probably doable. I can just about live on £10 per day in, say Cambodia. We'll see during the next four months what my daily spending *really* is here in the UK. If there's simply no way I can keep my daily spending down to £10, I'll increase it a little, maybe to £15 per day. We'll see.

Now I need to work out what streams of largely passive income I can actually generate!

And what do I mean by 'streams of largely passive income'?

Well, I want to do just enough income generating work to be able to meet my lifestyle goal - and no more. I want to have ample free time (not including income-earning activity such as writing) available to travel, enjoy nature, and set up and run my charity.

That dictates that the means by which I secure income must ultimately require as little effort from me as possible, yet continue to generate an income.

The ultimate form that takes is passive income. Creating something once that then generates an income without any, or at least with little, further effort. Digital projects is one obvious example. Music, books, software.

Write a decent song, sell it digitally into the future.

Write a software app and make it available in app stores on Apple and Android.

Write a book once, get it published, sit back and wait for people to buy it.

Or rather *write as many books as are needed* to meet a reasonable percentage of my income goal. I enjoy writing so, ultimately, it might be possible to write enough books to yield all the income I need.

But I'll be sensible and assume I'll need more than just books to sell. Books will be just one source of income. I need multiple things to sell from which to generate an income.

Another possibility is short courses. Create low cost short courses requiring no or little back end support. Publish them on online platforms. People pay for the course. I do nothing once the courses are created. That's essentially passive income. I'm not sure if that's possible but I'll explore and report back.

YouTube is another possible source of passive income. Create 'evergreen' videos on a YouTube channel and, once your channel is monetised, get a trickle of income from advertisers. And I *mean* a trickle!

Of the three sources of income described, books, courses and a monetised YouTube channel, videos on YouTube probably requires the most work for the least payoff. But a YouTube channel may well generate discoverability for the other two - the books and courses. I could feature my books within YouTube videos.

Although I like writing, I dislike being on video! So that might limit the extent to which my courses and videos appeal to my as-yet-undefined audiences.

Anyway, during this first four months of 2023 I'll experiment with two of those options. I'll attempt to write a book manuscript, and I'll build up a YouTube channel. I'll also look into the feasibility of creating a short course.

6 Two initial streams of income

I've decided to settle on two main income sources: selling books and monetising a YouTube channel. I'll look at short course creation and report back on that in the next volume of this book series.

Let's look at the skills and tools I'll need.

Book-writing seems more realistic, because I enjoy writing.

Monetising a YouTube channel seems a lot more challenging.

I suppose there's an opportunity cost: time spent setting up and creating videos for a YouTube channel might be better invested in writing more words for books.

In the next two sections I'll look in a bit more detail first at writing and independently publishing books, then at creating a YouTube channel.

7 Writing books

I enjoy writing blog posts. They're short and easy but they don't generate any income (although I should perhaps investigate whether a blog *can* generate another stream of cash!)

Writing long-form books is a far cry from writing short-form blog articles. Can I realistically write one, let alone a few, books?

And how does one actually generate income from a book? Isn't it impossible to find a publisher? Don't they take forever to actually publish a book once it's written?

Surely books aren't the way to *quickly* generate a stream of income? Especially not by the end of 2023!

Self-publishing has been an option for some time. I'm writing this very book with the intention of experimenting by publishing it myself. If you're reading it….I've succeeded!

Below, I'll give an overview of the process I anticipate following to get books written and published.

7.1 Going independent

The first decision I've made is to self-publish my books. I'll certainly not try to find a publisher to take them on.

I've been looking into book self-publishing for a while now.

Traditionally, one would draft a manuscript and then hand this over to the publisher to deal with the rest. The publisher would then do the editing, commission a professional book cover design, format the book, and then make it available for purchase in various formats.

As an independent author, I'm responsible for all of those steps.

I gather it's straightforward to commission freelancers to do steps such as manuscript editing and book cover design.

A quick sidenote here: *never*, I repeat *never*, sign up to one of those scammy self-publishing 'services'. They charge an exorbitant fee for doing tasks that you can readily do yourself or commission a freelancer to do at far, far lower cost. Those freelancers may well be digital nomads just like I aspire to be!

There are various sorts of editors, for example, and those editors can easily be found online and commissioned at reasonable rates.

So, decision taken: I'll be self publishing my books independently.

7.2 Getting manuscripts written

I've set myself the target of writing one book manuscript by the end of this spring season. I didn't specify the length of the manuscript. I forget that important detail!

Subsequent research convinced me to focus initially on tackling a ***short*** book writing project. This would enable me to learn how to get a book written, formatted and published. In theory, it'll yield an income sooner, because I can write it more quickly. But people will still need to purchase it, else it'll be a waste of time!

Binge-listening to some self publishing podcasts has given me an initial overview of the process, and confidence that it's a viable option.

I also purchased a couple of books on self-publishing. *Let's Get Digital* by David Gaughran is especially helpful. These together provide all one really needs to get started in independent publishing.

First challenge: by late 2023 and thereafter I plan to be abroad and traveling widely. This means the kit I use to write and publish books, both hardware and software, needs to suite a mobile, minimalist lifestyle.

First, the hardware.

As a digital nomad I can't use a desktop computer.

I also want to avoid using a laptop if at all possible. I have an M1 MacBook Air but I've decided to try not to use that for book-writing and publishing. It will eventually break. And, ideally, I'd like not to have to replace it.

Is it possible to go even smaller?

I have an iPad Air and an iPad Mini (don't ask! I clearly haven't yet embraced *digital* minimalism!). Oh, and I own an iPhone Mini 13…

My mind immediately turns to the iPad Mini and iPhone Mini. If I can write on those things alone, then clearly I can travel the world and write books anywhere!

Or can I?

I'm writing these words on my iPad Mini using a small keyboard case I found on Amazon via YouTube reviews. Here's an affiliate link to it on Amazon:

https://amzn.to/3J2SnFt

It's a tiny keyboard with a decent track-pad. It cost me £85. I've found the typing experience to be perfectly good and, combined with the iPad Mini, I've taken to writing with it in cafes and outside on the beach.

How about the iPhone Mini? Clearly I can't type on that for any length of time. How about dictation? A few years ago I had a go with expensive dictation software called Dragon Naturally Speaking. This gradually learns your voice using deep learning and converts your speech to text.

Voice to text technology has moved leaps and bounds since then. Basically the same functionality is built into the Apple (and Google) operating systems for free.

I experimented with voice-to-text on my iPhone Mini. It's brilliant!

It's no perfect. I've had to learn to very clearly enunciate words. But I've got better. By mid-March I was writing about 60% of my first-draft words for this book using this voice-to-text method on my iPhone Mini.

How about software? What am I actually writing into?

I ditched Microsoft Word some time ago for blog writing. You really shouldn't attempt to write longer-form books using traditional word processing software.

Instead, consider purchasing the specialist book-writing software called Scrivener. It costs under £50 for a lifetime licence for the iPad version and I think £25 for the iPhone version.

Scrivener basically does what a traditional word processing application will do, but it's written for long form writing. I.e. for book writing.

Because Scrivener book projects are automatically synced 'in the cloud' using Dropbox, I can easily switch between the iPhone and iPad to work on a given writing project.

For the book you're reading now, I've found myself sitting in a cafe each morning for a couple of hours, typing into the iPad Mini. I then switch to voice dictation on iPhone each afternoon. I can easily switch between the iPhone and the iPad and continue on with the same writing projects as long as I remember to synchronise in Dropbox.

I've found that I can type around 1000 words in about two hours each morning in the cafe, using the small keyboard and iPad Mini. I can write more quickly using voice dictation in the iPhone - about 1,500 words per hour.

Using voice to text takes a little getting used to but, once mastered, it's a revelation. I now walk along talking words into my phone. Yesterday I was sat on the beach doing the same. I have a favourite bench in the park where I sit and write by talking.

I'm going to experiment with using a lavaliere microphone rather than the microphone built into the iPhone. That might be better than having to hold the phone up to my face to write.

Just imagine: if I can readily write on the beach on the Isle of Wight, I can do the same on a beach in Bali! If I can write a book in my local park, I can write one in a Costa Rica National Park!

I wrote earlier that 'small is beautiful' when it comes to book-writing. If this current book project works out, I'll move on to writing a whole load of relatively short books. Book length will vary from as short and snappy as 10,000 words to 30,000 words or more.

If I can manage to write at least 1000 words per day, a 30,000 word rough draft should take about 30 days to write. I should be able to get more than 1000 words down each day though.

Right, what next? It's fine to draft manuscript. But how do I turn it into an actual book?

7.3 What about research?

Before we move on to the steps to publication, here's an interlude. The eagle-eyed amongst you will have noticed that what I've been suggesting so far appears to assume that what I want to write is already in my head.

That's basically true. But it's based on a fair amount of prior research and reading.

That's where the idea of writing a book entirely on a very small device like an iPhone runs into problems.

What if I'm out in the field, writing about conservation policy and advocacy? A lot of my inspiration comes from what I see in nature around me.

But I'm also planning on writing a few more technical books. Those require a deep dive into ecological evidence, journal articles, reports etc.

I read a lot of journal articles. Many of these are open access. These can be easily sent to the Kindle application that I have on my phone. Rather than download a PDF that's impossible to read effectively on an iPhone, I go to the article homepage on the publishers website. The article text displayed on the journal page can be sent straight to the Kindle from there. The Kindle then opens it as if it's a ebook. Although not all of the graphics and formulae are properly presented in the Kindle, the text itself is. And, for the purpose of my writing, that's what I need.

Grey literature articles and reports are more tricky. I tend to download these as PDFs from organisation websites. There are online applications that can be used to convert these into e-book files. They can then be read on the Kindle app. But the success of the conversion is often hit and miss.

It's far easier to conduct research using the iPad Mini. With this, you can use the split screen tool to view PDF documents and the Scrivener app side-by-side. Although both are rather small, I find them fine to work on. Another option, if you have both devices, would be to read on the iPad Mini, and use voice-to-text to take notes on the iPhone.

Much of what I'm writing in this book is knowledge I gained from trying things out, listening to podcasts, watching YouTube channels, and reading blog articles. All of that research can easily be done on either the iPhone or on the iPad Mini.

7.4 Getting the manuscript edited

I'm happy that I can write an initial manuscript largely on my iPad and iPhone Mini. No need for a laptop, less so a desktop.

Let's assume we have a finished, rough manuscript.

Ordinarily, one would hand this over to a publisher. They'd deal with getting it edited, formatted and published. I have no desire to find a publisher. I'm striving to be independent.

So I need first of all to sort out editing.

I gather from podcasts that it's straightforward to find and hire a freelance book editor. In fact, the big book publishers often use the same freelancers.

But this is my first book and I can't afford to hire an editor yet. I'm going to do the editing myself (so you *will* have found errors, for which I apologise. I'm grateful for the feedback!)

I'll start the editing process by re-reading the manuscript on my iPhone Mini and sorting out any errors I see. Then I'll do that again. I gather that an additional effective method is to read the manuscript out aloud. That's a good way of spotting missing words.

There are limits to how effective the author of a book can be in editing their own work. We have blind spots. We often fill-in missing words and thus fail to notice them. And, because we know what we meant to write, we often miss spelling errors or incorrect words.

Does this mean we do actually need to pay a professional editor?

What about editing software?

Grammarly seems popular. But Joanna Penn suggests ProWitingAid. This is a step-up from Grammarly and is getting better as artificial intelligence (AI) is integrated into it. It's expensive but there's an affordable monthly option.

So, for this book, I looked into purchasing a month licence for ProWritingAid. If I like it, I thought, and if I start to earn income from book sales, I'll invest in a lifetime licence.

But it looks like you can't use ProWritingAid on an iPad or iPhone.

We have a problem!

At the time of writing, I think I'll just rely on my own editing skills to get this manuscript finished. I'll explore other software editing options this summer and report on them in the next instalment of this series.

Assuming I manage to get the editing finished, I'll need to sort out the all-important book cover.

Then I'll need to get my finished manuscript and book cover combined and formatted as an actual book.

Let's look at those steps next.

7.5 Getting a book cover

Book covers are incredibly important. People really do judge a book by its cover. Be on in the shelf of a bookshop, or the virtual shelf of an online platform like Amazon, people scan and scroll through and tend to look at what catches their eye.

One of the first rules of independent publishing is: *don't attempt to design your own book cover*!

But commissioning book cover designer to do this is relatively expensive.

For this book, I'm going to ignore all the advice. I'm going to try to design my own book cover.

Luckily I can use the free software package Canva. This is the same piece of software I now use to design my YouTube channel video thumbnails.

There are other excellent bits of software and applications you can use to design your own book covers. I have very little patience. I know how Canva works. So I'm going to use that.

Canva has a range of templates that you can adapt to create a book cover. Some of these are available with a free subscription. Some are only available with a paid subscription. I only have a free subscription.

Canva also offers a blank canvas with which you can build your own book cover elements.

The cover of the book you're reading now was designed by me using a blank canvas in Canva.

I'll have to await book sales data to see if it's a help or hindrance! I may come back later, assuming I get a small amount of income, and commissioned a professional freelance designer. We'll see.

Right, what next?

I need to get my manuscript formatted and all bundled together for publication.

How?

7.6 Book formatting

A key principle for independently publishing books is to learn as you go along. Don't try to learn every step upfront.

And I don't yet know how I'm going to format my books! At the time of writing, mid February 2023, I've done some background reading and listened to some podcasts. These have given me a rough idea that it's straightforward to turn a finished manuscript into files formatted for ebook and print-on-demand paperback and hardcover books.

All I can do at this stage is mention what they say. In the next volume of this series of books, I will be able to give a full account of what I've actually done to format the book you're reading now.

There are several pieces of book formatting software you can use. One popular option is Draft2Digital. This company is a distributor. That means you can upload your book to their platform, get it formatted there, and they will distribute it to a variety of online retail stores. Basically, you can upload your finished book manuscript and run it through their free formatting tool. You can then download the formatted e-book file. I gather this option is rather limited on what you can do once your manuscript is formatted. You can't really tweak the formatted file. But it's free and easy.

That's one option. There are several others.

Amazon offers perhaps the most straightforward approach. I gather you can use that approach when you come to uploading your book file to Amazon for publication.

And that's what we'll look at next.

7.7 Getting your e-book published on Amazon

I've not yet published a book at the time of writing this. So I'm only going to give the very briefest of outlines here.

Basically, the best long term approach appears to be to publish wide, on as many online platforms as possible.

This means, generally speaking, don't publish the e-book version on Kindle Unlimited (KU). KU is part of the Amazon Kindle Direct Publishing (KDP) Select programme. KDP Select demands exclusivity. That means, if your e-book is enlisted into KDP Select and in KU, you can't publish the e-book version on any other platform for the 90 day term of the agreement. You can go ahead and publish paperback, hardcover, and audiobook versions on Amazon and elsewhere however.

What shall I do?

For my first book, I'm going to ignore the mainstream advice within the self published book community. I'm going to sign up to Amazon KDP Select and enroll this book into Kindle Unlimited for an initial 90 day agreement period.

After 90 days, I can either sign up for another 90 days, or remove the e-book from KDP Select and publish it more widely.

I've looked at a million YouTube videos on how to do this. These are the steps:

- create an Amazon KDP account, using your existing Amazon customer account if you have one

- Export the completed manuscript from Scrivener as a docx document into a file on your computer

- log into your Amazon KDP account

- Press the create new book button

- opt to create an e-book

- fill in the various boxes as requested

- upload the completed docx format manuscript and book cover PDF when requested

- use the previewer to check whether Amazon has correctly formatted your manuscript into e-book form

- Set your desired pricing when prompted to do so

- Press submit

That, in highly condensed form, is basically it. Amazon now has your completed e-book documents and will check these to make sure everything is in order. After a few hours or a day or two, assuming there are no problems, your ebook will appear on Amazon for sale.

Now, that's a very rough account of what I anticipate I will need to do when it comes to publishing the book you're reading now.

It's probably a bit more complicated than that, but everyone says it's actually rather straightforward.

Once I have an e-book published, I'll go back and attempt to publish a paperback version. I'm not sure if I'll attempt to publish an audiobook. And I don't think it's worth publishing a hardcover version of a very short book like this. But we'll see.

7.8 Writing on the move: Concluding wrap up

The above account give us a brief overview of what I anticipate to be my book writing and initial e-book publishing process. It all seems pretty tractable. In terms of the key question: can

I write books, publish them and earn a worthwhile income from writing as a nomad, the answer appears to be potentially, yes. The initial steps of actually getting the manuscript drafted and then fully edited seem the most challenging. Once I have a completed manuscript, the subsequent steps of book cover creation, manuscript formatting, and publishing itself, appear very straightforward. Although few experienced self-publishers would attempt to create their own book covers, it's extremely straightforward to create something purporting to be a book cover using the free Canva app on a phone or tablet computer.

Alternatively, it's easy to find and work with a freelance book cover designer.

In short, writing and independently publishing books 'on the move' appears to be one of the easier ways to earn money as a location independent travel-junkie.

8 Creating and monetising a YouTube channel

This option seems a lot less convincing than book-writing as an early income generator.

But, given that I'll be using a YouTube channel partly to promote my books anyway, it's worth exploring YouTube monetisation.

Setting up a YouTube channel is relatively straightforward. I've actually had one since 2014. Up until very recently, I was just uploading fairly pointless videos. It was only in February 2023 that I started to use my initial YouTube channel as a writer platform. I subsequently set up another channel, and I also recuperated an earlier vanlife focused channel.

8.1 What's the focus of your YouTube channel?

If, like me, you have a YouTube channel to which you upload random videos with no particular purpose, you can probably forget about monetisation.

If, on the other hand, you intend to use it more professionally, as a platform and a way to generate some income, it could potentially be quite useful.

8.2 How do you Monetise a YouTube channel?

At the time of writing this in February 2023, I possess only a rudimentary understanding of YouTube channels.

I will be investigating this subject in more detail throughout 2023. Later books in the series will set out what I learn.

For now, my main task is to attempt to monetise the channel, by which I currently mean qualify for Google AdSense.

YouTube adds adverts onto some of your videos regardless of your own monetisation status.

Until you qualify for Google AdSense, you don't benefit from those adverts. To monetise your channel through Google AdSense you need to meet the requirements set out by YouTube. You need 1000 subscribers and 10,000 hours of video watch time.

Once you reach those requirements, and assuming you're accepted for monetisation, you will receive a cut of the fee paid by advertisers to place adverts on YouTube.

I don't know how this works in detail at this stage. I know the payment rates vary widely. Advertisers pay a lot more to place ads on videos in certain niches. My guess is that for owners of YouTube channels producing videos on writing, advertisers pay very little to place adverts. This presumably means that the income I receive from those ads will be correspondingly very small. If my YouTube channel featured videos reviewing expensive tech equipment, I assume the cut I would receive from adverts would be rather higher.

My current guess is that I might receive a few pennies monthly from Google AdSense once monetised. But we'll have to see.

8.3 Setting up the YouTube channel account

You'll need to set up a Google account and a Gmail address if you don't already have one. You use your Gmail address to log in and set the YouTube account up.

Because YouTube is owned by Google which also owns Gmail, setting up your own YouTube account is straightforward. You simply log into YouTube using your Gmail address and go from there. The platform walks you through the process. It's very easy.

8.4 Formatting your YouTube channel

According to some tutorials on, erm, YouTube, it's possible to set up your YouTube channel in a way that best presents you.

First, you can create your own image to stretch along the banner space at the top of your channel.

I designed a very basic banner image using Canva. Again, there are tutorials on YouTube explaining how to do this. You're also able to add little hot link buttons into the banner that direct people to other social media accounts such as LinkedIn and Twitter. These buttons are easily added as you set your channel up or subsequently.

I also set up Playlists. At the time of writing, in mid-April, I've not done much more than that.

I'll be exploring additional optimisation elements over the summer and in the next volume of this book.

8.5 Creating videos for YouTube

At the moment, I simply use my iPhone Mini 13 to shoot all of my YouTube videos. I use it in landscape mode to shoot longer videos, and in portrait mode to shoot Short videos under one minute long. These shorter form videos are aimed at the YouTube Shorts shelf. This relatively new element of YouTube seems to be designed to compete with the short form vertical video format pioneered by TikTok.

I use the free iMovie app from Apple to turn my individual video shots into longer videos to be uploaded.

Short videos can simply be uploaded with minimal fuss or presentation. Although I will come back to this, because this format of video is developing its own design language too.

Longer form videos, longer than one minute, can be given a thumbnail. A YouTube video thumbnail is probably best thought of as equivalent to a book cover. It's also like a tap on the shoulder. If it stands out, a potential viewer of the video gets that tap on the shoulder. If it doesn't stand out they won't.

So you want to create a thumbnail for each video that stands out and is attractive to the viewer you're aiming in your video at.

For me, that means I want my videos to stand out to writers, and more specifically, those thinking about self publishing their books.

I use Canva to design my thumbnails. I use my own photographs, again taken using my iPhone Mini 13. Although Canva offers a range of YouTube thumbnail templates, I tend to use a blank template and add elements to it. I upload my photograph. Then I add text. I colour the text so it stands out. It needs to be fairly large. You don't want people squinting to read what is written on the thumbnail. They won't. The focus will be drawn to a nearby thumbnail that does stand out and is easy to read. Minimise the number of words on a thumbnail.

As I'm uploading my video to YouTube it will invite me to add a thumbnail. I then simply upload the thumbnail created using Canva.

I then add a very simple title to the video. And I write a slightly longer description. I haven't yet learnt about search engine optimisation. So my video titles and descriptions are probably rubbish. Over this summer I'll be doing some research on how to do this properly and I'll report that in the next volume of this book series.

8.6 YouTube: concluding wrap up

Okay. I now have a YouTube channel. It's very basic, and I only have 88 subscribers as of the end of April 2023. I'll be exploring how to improve it and I'll write more detail in the summer volume of this book series. I should stress that at the time of writing I've only looked at one method of earning income via a YouTube channel: Google AdSense.

But I gather there are other ways to drive an income from videos on YouTube. One that I'm about to start exploring is affiliate marketing. I'll explore that in the next book.

9 The Breaking Free Diaries

The following section is comprised a diary I've kept during the spring season of Breaking Free in 2023. This section is rather light because I didn't write entries that frequently. I'll be writing near-daily diary entries during the Summer Season and they'll appear in the next volume of this series.

January 2023

Tuesday 3rd January 2023

New Year, new beginning - I hope! Today properly marks the start of my attempt to become fully location-independent

An early task for me is to further minimise my possessions. I've made some decent progress. Over the last winter, what remained of my large book collection was being stored in a friend's house. I collected these in early January and stuck them in my van. I then drove from the Isle of Wight to Falmouth in Cornwall in order to deposit these books at the university campus, where I knew the large student community would eagerly take them.

I wear prescription glasses and so my next priority is sorting out an alternative. I'm squeamish, so the idea of laser eye surgery isn't appealing. I've nonetheless booked an eye test to see if it's an option. I'll try out contact lenses too. If contact lenses don't work for me, I'll look again at the laser, and, if all else fails, I'll resort to a new pair of glasses.

Thursday 19th January

OK, so looking at the state of my bank account, it's clear that I haven't got enough of a financial 'runway' saved to keep me going until books and the YouTube channels start to yield income.

So I'm going to start looking for short-term, part-time work to top up the bank account and by myself some more freedom.

February 2023

Friday 10th February

I had a BC job interview at the beginning of the week. They say they'll let people know on Monday. It's full-time so ideally I'll not get the job! But it would be an effective way of topping up the bank account more quickly.

I've finally added a 'Wild Writer' playlist to my main, personal YouTube channel. I figure it's best to host my writing videos there rather than create yet another, separate, dedicated writing YouTube channel. I might be wrong. I've uploaded a couple of writing 'vlogs' so far and will try to upload daily. I can tweet those. I did earlier and it had zero effect on views! I have only one or two views….

Eventually that writing Playlist will be a venue through which I promote the Writers in the Wild book and associated short course. I'm hoping I'll eventually make a bit of income from AdSense, the short course and, of course, the book. I must get on with the book!

I did make some good progress with my cultured meat book yesterday. So far today I've done no writing at all.

Apart from 183 words written here, of course.

Friday 17th February
My extreme minimalism - a precursor to fully breaking free - continues to ratchet up. I've

purchased the world's smallest telescope! And a new pair of low-cost, compact binoculars. Adding kit, not removing it. But absolute essentials for a minimalist birder.

Monday 20ᵗʰ February

I finally purchased a website account and launched my personal website - stevecjones.uk - last night! I've been working on it this morning. Taking shape nicely.

I'm not entirely sure what role it'll play, or how I'll monetise it. I guess it's the platform through which I'll promote my books and YouTube channels.

Tuesday 21ˢᵗ February

Good progress. My main website is really taking shape. I've posted three new Rewilding pieces in the Natural Areas blog, one backed with a short YouTube video I linked to from the blog post. So I can drive traffic to my main YouTube channel. I need to work out how to do the opposite. I've tweeted out those pieces and that works well, with the photo I include with each article forming the thumbnail on the tweet.

The What Bird? YouTube channel is getting views and has fifty subscribers as I write this. But I can't see how I'll ever monetise that channel. My main writing Youtube channel still has only 25 subscribers, but I've not been promoting it. I can see a route to monetising that one.

I think I need to focus on the main writing YouTube channel and blog. And the vanlife channel, which I think I can also monetise if I really push content on it.

Wednesday 22nd February

A couple more books dumped on the university campus 'free' shelf, and two picked up from Amazon locker! I'm not supposed to be buying more physical books…

My What Bird? YouTube channel now has 56 subscribers; my main channel still stagnant at 25. Given that Shorts drove subscribers on the Bird channel, I think I need to post a few more on the main channel. I posted two today: one has 11 views, the other has 2 views this evening!

I need a much clearer YouTube game plan. Only three channels appear worth considering:

- The main writing channel
- What Bird?
- Cornish Vandweller

I wonder which of those three presents the best opportunity for Adsense monetisation?

Sunday 26th February

It's so chilly! And it's set to get colder in the first week in March. I'll be back on the Isle of Wight by then. I'll hopefully get some writing done there…. (I recall writing that I'm looking forward to getting writing done when I get back to Falmouth, a few months ago! The grass is always greener…)

Monday 27th February

OK, so what are my Breaking Free priorities for this week? I've shifted my What Birds? Shorts content posting from its dedicated channel to my main writing channel. And I'm going to start to create Breaking Free content for a playlist on my van-dwelling channel. I'll put it there rather than on my main channel because the main one is really about writing and rewilding - it's my main author channel alongside my author website.

I've ordered a Jetboil Flash, the main reason being that I'll be able to boil water and warm soup a lot faster in the back on the van, ultimately saving money on gas. Hopefully I'll gas myself less that way too!

I'm essentially narrowing my YouTube channels down to two: my main writing one, and the van-dwelling one. Rationalising in this way concentrates watch time, hopefully increasing the possibility of monetisation.

It's going to be a slog, YouTube.

So writing at least three books is the higher priority. I did manage to get some work done on the Writers in the Wild book yesterday.

March 2023

Wednesday 6th March
I wrote 300 words this morning but am focussed on getting the van ready for the drive back to the Isle of Wight.

Saturday 18th March

Back on the Isle of Wight. I just uploaded a video on my Writer YouTube channel about St Lawrence - a favoured writing and birding spot.

Tuesday 28th March

Still on the Isle of Wight. Actually made some progress this morning!

I did a quick search for basic Canva tutorials. Canva is a user-friendly graphic design tool one can use for free to create nice YouTube thumbnails and banners. They also have book cover templates…I found one guy with a tutorial on using it on your phone. So I downloaded the app onto my iPhone Mini 13 and had a go at designing a very basic book cover on my phone. It turned out to be pretty straightforward.

It's been a while since I noted on my YouTube channel data, so here goes:

Writers in the wild:
- Subscribers, 43

Van life:

- Subscribers, 49

That feels like the main two channels. So they're very slowly creeping up. I'll double-down on those two.

Elon Musk is doing something weird with Twitter. It appears that it's going entirely subscription based. If you're not a subscriber, you'll become undiscoverable. Because I'm not willing to subscribe, that basically kills it as a platform of any value to me.

I have over 2000 subscribers on Twitter. So it'll be a shame to lose it as a means of communication. It just means I need to double-down on my own author website platform and on YouTube. Assuming YouTube doesn't also downplay non-subscribers.

April 2023

Saturday 1st April
Had a rare event: a 'quick birding walk around Ventnor East Cliffs' longer video has

amassed 44 views in two days! I never get more than a trickle of views on longer videos. I also got one more subscriber on the back of that video: we're at 45...

Monday 3rd April

I had a play with ChatGPT to see how well it generates non-fiction text from basic prompts. It certainly generates decent sentences, and the essence of the natural history information presented appeared essentially correct. It clearly could provide a good starting point for quickly generating very rough drafts of blog posts. By 'rough drafts' I mean decent sentences requiring thorough fact-checking and referencing. I can't see myself using it any time soon, because it seems to me to suck the joy out of the writing process.

Wednesday 5th April

I've got another subscriber on my main channel - 46! Good grief, this is hard going....

I've uploaded several birding videos with what look to me like reasonable thumbnails. All videos will have thumbnails going forward.

Sunday 8th April

I'm actually making really good progress!

So much so that I'm becoming increasingly confident that my writing and YouTube channel exploits may actually work. I just haven't really yet defined exactly what that would look like!

Wednesday 12th April

I had an excellent writing day on the 10th - 1,200 words - but nothing at all yesterday. I did manage to get a Birding at Wheelers Bay video posted, with a nice thumbnail designed in Canva. Unfortunately I don't really know what 'nice' means from a viewer's point of view. That video only has 12 views as of now but I feel the long-form videos might be gaining a bit of momentum.

I do have a bit of a dilemma regarding what exactly my main YouTube channel niche is. Currently it's three sub-niches: birding, writing and rewilding. Most videos are birding, a couple on writing, none yet on rewilding.

I think what I'll do going forward is to combine either writing or rewilding chatter into bird walk videos. That could work quite well. I have a walk, birding, and updating on writing progress, or covering some rewilding topic, as I go. That kind of fits the 'Writer in the Wild' theme quite nicely: out in the wild, talking about writing. Or rewilding.

I'll need to think about how to design thumbnails that make it clear what each video is actually about.

Friday 14th April

My main YouTube writer channel is slowly growing, now standing at 64 subscribers. Getting to a thousands subscribers and four thousand hours of watch time seems a long way off. But my subscriber count has double in the last thirty days roughly.

Sunday 16th April

My writer channel subscriber count stands at 65. Edging up….

I uploaded a longer 'how I self-publish nature books' video yesterday. It's had five views! I've posted a link to that on LinkedIn.

I've written about 500 words so far this morning. It's 11.30am.

Wednesday 19th April

My subscriber count on my main writing YouTube channel has climbed to 68.

I've started a new experimental YouTube channel called the iPhone Entrepreneur. I started this yesterday, and the subscriber count already stands at 15.

Writing is going well. This is pretty exciting. Given how much I enjoy writing I don't think there is much doubt that I can make this work as a long-term living.

Friday 21st April

My writer YouTube channel subscriber number now stands at 70!

My vanlife channel has even grown by one subscriber, to 50...

The experimental iPhone Entrepreneur YouTube channel remains at 15 subscribers.

I did a little bit of writing this morning. Mostly rejigging a couple of books. I've managed to design a book cover for my Shrublands book. I actually think I might use that cover. And that might be the first book I get published.

Abbie, the person who owns what is my favourite tearoom, suggested recording audios from my writing and uploading those to the YouTube channel. It's quite a genius idea to be honest. It might help to increase the watch time, especially people listen to the end.

So later I might experiment by narrating one of my blog posts.

Saturday 22nd April

The writer channel subscriber count sits at 72. The van life count remains at 50. And that for the iPhone Entrepreneur channel sits at 15.

Sunday 23rd April

Reasonable progress with writing this morning. I wrote about 450 words. I also started to edit the early chapters of one of my books.

My writing YouTube channel subscribe account stands at 74. I haven't a clue how I gained two subscribers since yesterday!

Tuesday 25th April

Oddly, I had a small flurry of subscribers! It now stands at 79 on my main writing channel.

Thursday 27th April

My Writing YouTube channel sits at 82 subscribers. I've not done a great deal of writing over the last week. I really must decide which of several books I'll publish first and get the damned thing finished! I'll be able to sort out the boring publishing things - getting it onto Amazon etc - once I have a finished manuscript.

Then I can move on to the second.

Friday 28th April

My writing YouTube channel sits at 88 subscribers. I'm gaining one or two daily on average. I think I'm probably gaining most of these from Shorts. All of my Shorts are about birding (well, bird identification). Not an ideal audience for what's supposed to be my writer's platform!

Sunday 30th April

Well then, here we are. The last day of spring 2023. The last day of season one of my attempts to Break Free.

I spent this morning in the café as usual. Thankfully, I was able to write around 800 words. That represents a good morning at the moment. I usually get disturbed by friends wanted to chat. Not this morning.

Tomorrow we enter Season Two. Now I need to turn my attention to getting this Season One book published!

10 End of season one

Well, it's now the end of April 2023 and time to take stock.

How are things going in general, and what kind of progress am I making against the Goal, targets and activities I set myself?

As I write this, I'm sitting in my van in Ventnor on the Isle of Wight. Over the last week, at the end of April 2023, I've really got back into the flow of writing. And I've been producing daily videos for my main writing YouTube channel.

On a good day, I've been writing about 1000 words. On average, I've probably been writing about 700 words per day. I usually achieve that in about two hours of more or less concerted writing effort.

Clearly, two hours of writing is way less that I can achieve if I really put my mind to this.

I really need to pull my fingers out!

Towards the end of the period covered in this book, I created a new experimental YouTube channel, *The iPhone Entrepreneur*. What's that all about? Well, the idea is to experiment with creating passive income using just my iPhone Mini 13.

It's an interesting concept. I think that a YouTube channel focused on building a business using a smartphone might attract a reasonable sized subscriber base. And, because it deals with both technology, the iPhone, or the smartphone more generally, and side hustles and building a location independent business, the adverts that are placed on the channel may attract a reasonably high AdSense payment rate. I'm not sure why I think that might be true.

I was surprised that I got 12 subscribers in the first day on my iPhone channel. Equally surprising is that the Shorts I've uploaded on the iPhone channel are getting reasonable numbers of views, but the single long form video I've uploaded still hasn't had any views at all!

10.1 Did I meet my Season 1 targets?

To recap, here are the targets I set myself back in January for this Spring Season on Breaking Free in 2023:

Target 1.1: Complete one book manuscript

Target 1.2: 100 subscribers on my writing YouTube channel

Target 1.3: Reduce spending to £10/day

Target 1.4: Write a more detailed delivery plan to demonstrate how it's possible to be in a position to live in the tropics from mid-November 2023.

Let's look at each in turn:

Target 1.1: Complete one book manuscript

In short, I've narrowly missed this target.

Well, I'm not far off having several manuscripts sorted. But that's part of my problem: I keep flitting between manuscripts!

I need to prioritise. List the various book projects in order of priority and focus on one book manuscript at a time.

Right now, a priority book is one that can be written quickly and so will begin to generate at least some kind of income. Longer form passion projects are not a priority right now!

I also need to write a lot more each day and I have for most of this first season. I've tended to write for just an hour or two each morning. I've usually written several hundred words to 1000 words that way.

I've also thoroughly embraced voice to text writing. Now, I can write in my iPhone Mini straight into Scrivener. I simply bring up the keyboard, activate the built-in dictation facility, and talk. If it's breezy, this approach doesn't work. So I plug in a lavaliere microphone. That's been working very well.

I need to talk the grammar as I'm writing this way. This was a bit awkward at first, but I'm now fully in the swing of it.

Target 1.2: 100 subscribers on my writing YouTube channel

My subscriber count stands at 88. Given the growth I've seen during April (a doubling) I'll take that as a near-miss rather than a fail. I've put more effort into getting my YouTube channel sorted out than focusing on one book manuscript and getting it written. I'm not sure what that means really.

Target 1.3: Reduce spending to £10/day

Complete fail! I spent around £20/day between January-April. My profligate spending means I've almost used up my savings, increasing the need to get some part-time work. That wasn't the idea!

So I'll make a concerted effort to bring spending down during the Summer Season.

Target 1.4: Write a more detailed delivery plan to demonstrate how it's possible to be in a position to live in the tropics from mid-November 2023.

I've made no progress on this pretty important task (I did add it towards the end of the last month, April!). I'll shift it into the Summer Season and get it done in early May.

So, there we go. In a moment I'll set some targets for Season 2 - the summer season, May-

August 2023. First, I'll draw attention to a few of lessons.

10.2 Some lessons

I've learnt a fair amount during the first four months of 2023. Here are some of the more important lessons.

<u>Building a YouTube following takes time</u>

My subscriber number grew at a glacial pace between January and April. I started to use customised thumbnails on my longer videos but this has had little discernible effect on subscriber growth. Most subscribers appear to have come from Shorts (videos under one minute that appear on the YouTube Shorts shelf). But I've not yet learnt how to interpret the data provided by YouTube in the analytics accessible via YouTube Studio: i'll add that to my tasks list!

Many creators strive to satisfy the criteria required to qualify for the YouTube Partner Programme. This unlocks monetisation via Google Adsense (where one receives a small payment from adds that appear on their videos).

But, depending on one's niche and skill in creating content, this form of monetisation can take an awfully long time to yield a pitifully small amount of money.

<u>In the early days at least, writing and publishing books will probably yield an income quicker than monetising a YouTube channel via AdSense</u>

First, it's important to note that a YouTube channel can be an excellent platform through which to promote books you're writing. So although there is an opportunity cost, meaning your time might be better spent writing books than populating a YouTube channel, they're not mutually exclusive.

So I've revised my expectations. I now see the YouTube channel as a means of building a following. Some of my followers might go on to purchase my books once they're published.

<u>But there are other ways to monetise a YouTube channel irrespective of subscriber numbers</u>

The previous lesson really only refer to monetising via AdSense. That's the Google advert placement mechanism through which advertising revenue is shared with content creators.

In addition to this, YouTube provides a platform on which you can promote products you use and like and gain a sort of commission if your viewers go on to buy that product having seen it on your channel, using a special affiliate link.

During the summer season I'll be looking into this more closely. I gather the Amazon Affiliate Programme is one means of gaining additional income irrespective of channel subscriber count. I'll report on this in the next volume of this book series.

It really is possible to draft a book manuscript on a mobile phone using voice to text

This was probably my most impactful discovery. Although I failed in my bid to complete a manuscript by the end of the spring season, by the end of April, I did get very close to it. And that's manuscript was written largely using the voice to text functionality within my iPhone Mini.

Much of this book has also been written in the same way. This entry specifically is being written via voice to text while I'm sat at a café on Ventnor beach on the Isle of Wight. We will discover during the summer season, and in the next volume of this book series, just how much further than drafting a manuscript I can go using a mobile phone.

I've already started to edit the manuscript of that first book and I have to say I'm finding that making corrections using the keyboard on the phone, and adding bits of text using voice to text, is very easy and satisfying. Can one go even further than drafting a manuscript and editing it? I will explore that over the summer.

You need to set realistic daily spending targets

I set myself the ludicrous target of restricting my expenditure to £10 per day.

Few normal people in the real world can live so frugally. All I can say here is that you should set a target based on your own particular circumstances and lifestyle choices. It is very likely that you spend more money than you need to to lead a fully satisfying life. I'm a rather extreme example, having set about turning myself into a minimalist generating a location independent income.

I'm nowhere near achieving my £10 a day maximum spend target. I might run through some sums in the next volume (summer season) of this book series to test what's possible. That book will be published in early September 2023.

Have a financial runway

I started out with very modest savings in the bank. Those savings have proved insufficient to see me through the process of setting up income streams via book sales and the YouTube channel. I'm therefore job hunting.

Don't get lulled into a false sense of security. Having money in the bank dampened my effort. It made me feel too relaxed. I've not put as much effort into writing as I needed to. I've learned from this mistake and hopefully you will be able to build up a sufficient sum of money in the bank to finance your own bid to break free. Probably, around £15,000 is what I really needed in the bank to feel comfortable. I didn't have that. And so I need to find some work.

So they are the main lessons learned during the first season of my bid to Break Free in 2023.

Many of the lessons drawn above point in one direction: I needed a proper business plan for this venture. I needed to evaluate properly its viability. What viability would look like. I've added this requirement into my summer season and will set it out in the book covering that period.

10.3 Targets for Season Two

It's the end of April and Season One is just about over. Here, I'll set some targets for the summer season. That's another four months, May to the end of August.

<u>Target 2.1</u>: Complete four book manuscripts

Given that I failed to achieve my modest target to complete one manuscript in Season One, aspiring, sorry, committing, to complete that one, and another three, seems a stretch.

But I think it's realistic.

I have that first book all-but finished. I have a couple half-way there. I'm also writing the book you're reading now! I'm confident…

I've come to appreciate just how quickly you can write using voice to text. Although the accuracy isn't perfect, neither is it when I'm physically typing using my fingers. Both approaches generate errors. The two sets of errors probably cancel each other out.

The two big benefits of writing using voice to text, being able to write walking around, and not being plagued by spelling mistakes, oh, and of course the much faster writing rate, to me make this the preferred approach to writing.

And I am an enthusiastic writer. I don't find the writing process traumatic. I have quite a few book ideas.

<u>Target 2.2</u>: Publish those four books

Assuming I do actually manage to complete four manuscripts, I'll be able to move on to learning the arts of editing, book cover design, formatting and publication. No small set of tasks, but I'm up for it! I set out a very rough overview of the process earlier in this book. I will need to turn to actually making each of those steps real. And I'm beginning to think I might get a lot of the way to the publication Mark purely using my iPhone 13 Mini.

<u>Target 2.3</u>: 300 subscribers on my writing YouTube channel

It's hard to say if this is possible. My subscriber count stood at 88 at the end of April. Gaining 212 in the four months of summer 2023 might be pushing it. But even that number is only 30% of the way to getting monetised in terms of subscriber count. We'll see.

<u>Target 2.4</u>: Reduce spending to £10/day

I really, really must meet this target! Most of my spending is on coffee in cafes. I have to moderate this. I own a jet boil flash. That sits in my van. I can easily boil that to make a coffee or tea whenever I want. There's no excuse.

Target 2.4: Write a more detailed delivery plan to demonstrate how it's possible to be in a position to live in the tropics from mid-November 2023.

Crucial 'proof of concept'. I need to set down the pathway for getting to my end goals for 2023. These sub-targets make little sense unless I know they all lead to meeting the main, end of year goal.

10.4 What now?

I can now relax a little. Season one is finished. I'm currently, on the last day of April 2023, nowhere near having any kind of side income. My savings have almost been used up. But I feel well on the way to achieving something at least.

Tomorrow, is the 1st May 2023 and the start of my summer season.

I'm now heading for the beach, where I'm going to carry on writing my book!

11 Conclusion

And so ends the first instalment of my book series *Breaking Free in 2023*. I'm not sure how much closer I am to achieving my overall goal of being able to live anywhere in the world on passive income by late in 2023.

But I think I've made good progress.

I managed to get one book manuscript almost completed by the end of April. My YouTube channels are up and running. And I'm exploring additional sources of income.

I'm now in the process of recording the next season. That's May, June, July and August 2023. The summer season. I've set myself another set of stretching targets. I'll have a better idea come August about whether my overall goal is possible.

You'll have to wait until the next book in the series is published in early September 2023 to find out how I do this summer!

12 Equipment and Further reading

Equipment

What gear have I used to write this book and create my YouTube channels? Here's a list:

iPhone Mini 13: https://amzn.to/43IsIcO
iPad Mini 6: https://amzn.to/3C9MVfZ
Scrivener writing software:
https://www.literatureandlatte.com/scrivener-affiliate.html?fpr=steve88

Books to read

Here's a list of a small number of books I found extremely useful during spring 2023.

Books about YouTube:
Tube Ritual: https://amzn.to/45NLVvC
YouTube Formula: https://amzn.to/3qsxUU8
YouTube Secrets: https://amzn.to/45DaN9k

Books about writing:
Let's Get Digital: https://amzn.to/3N9kgOA

How to Make a Living with your Writing:
https://amzn.to/3IU79OC
Write your Book on the Side:
https://amzn.to/3IV2Um0

The links above are all affiliate links.

13 About the author

Calvin Jones is a pen name. I live on the Isle of Wight in England and worked in the nature conservation sector for over two decades. In 2018 I moved into a small van, and, in January 2023 I hatched a plan to become completely location independent. I am in the process of setting up a small nature conservation charity focused on helping communities in tropical countries to establish local tropical nature reserves.

This is the first in a series of four books that'll record my efforts to build multiple streams of income that'll support my nomadism and location-independent lifestyle.

Sonia Choquette
How to make an
alchemy box ♡

Printed in Great Britain
by Amazon